3/03

P9-EFJ-141

Rookie
Read-About® Science

Living on a
Space Shuttle

By Carmen Bredeson

Consultants
Minna Gretchen Palaquibay
Rose Center for Earth and Space
American Museum of Natural History
New York, New York

Nanci Vargus, Ed.D.
Primary Multiage Teacher
Decatur Township Schools
Indianapolis, Indiana

Martha Walsh
Reading Specialist

Children's Press®
A Division of Scholastic Inc.
New York   Toronto   London   Auckland   Sydney
Mexico City   New Delhi   Hong Kong
Danbury, Connecticut

Designer: Herman Adler Design
Photo Researcher: Caroline Anderson
The photo on the cover shows astronaut Loren J. Shriver trying to catch
weightless candy while aboard the Space Shuttle *Atlantis*.

Library of Congress Cataloging-in-Publication Data

Bredeson, Carmen.
  Living on a space shuttle / by Carmen Bredeson.
    p. cm. — (Rookie read-about science)
Summary: Provides a simple description of how astronauts aboard a space
shuttle perform everyday activities such as eating, drinking, and sleeping.
Includes index.
  ISBN 0-516-22528-6 (lib. bdg.)   0-516-26955-0 (pbk.)
  1. Manned space flight—Juvenile literature. 2. Space flight—
Physiological effect—Juvenile literature. 3. Life support systems
(Space environment)—Juvenile literature. [1. Manned space flight.
2. Astronauts. 3. Space shuttles.] I. Title. II. Series.
  TL793.B7296 2003
  629.45—dc21
                                  2002011304

CHILDREN'S PRESS, AND ROOKIE READ-ABOUT®,
and associated logos are trademarks and or registered trademarks
of Grolier Publishing Co., Inc. SCHOLASTIC and associated logos
are trademarks and or registered trademarks of Scholastic Inc.

1 2 3 4 5 6 7 8 9 10 R 11 10 09 08 07 06 05 04 03

Living in space is not like living on Earth. Everything floats in space.

Astronauts do not walk in the space shuttle. They float from place to place. A push on the wall gets them going.

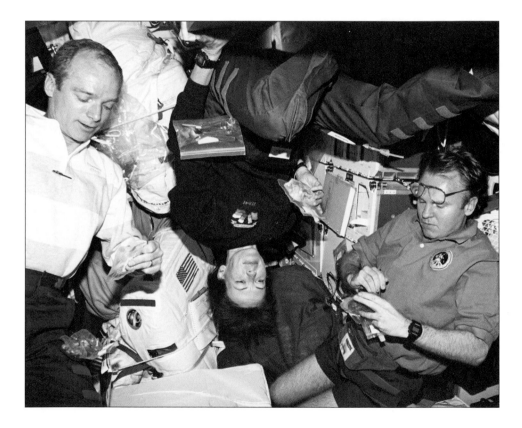

There is no up or down on the shuttle. Being on the ceiling feels the same as being on the floor.

Food floats, too. The food
the astronauts eat comes
in cans or packets so it
does not float away.

9

Water and juice are in drink pouches. Astronauts sip them from a straw.

At least swallowing works the same in space. Food is pushed into the stomach by muscles in the throat.

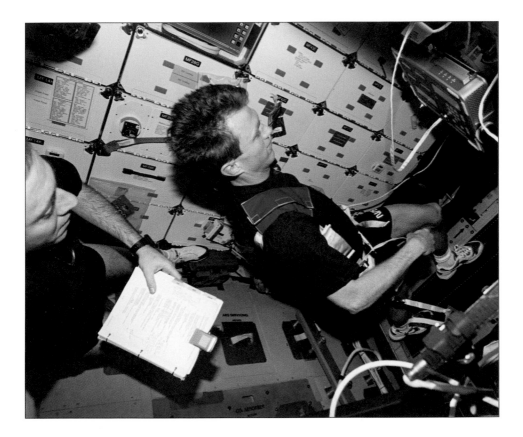

14

Floating around is much easier than walking.

The crew has to exercise to stay strong. The astronauts work up a sweat on a treadmill.

There is no shower or sink on the shuttle. The water would float away.

The crew washes with damp cloths or wet wipes.

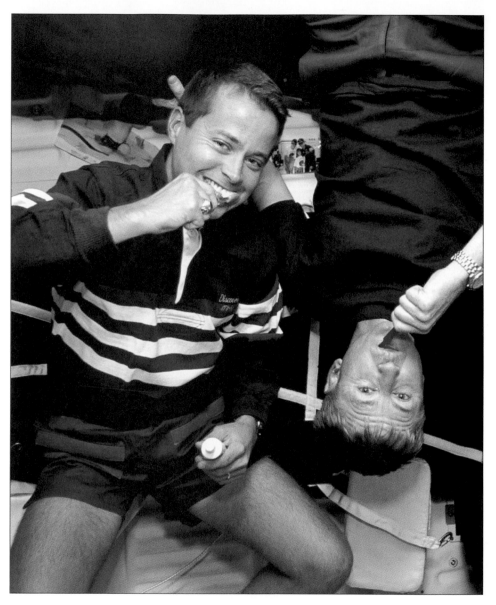

It is easy for astronauts
to keep their teeth
clean. Toothpaste sticks
to toothbrushes.

Astronauts can even brush
their teeth upside down!

The shuttle toilet works like a vacuum cleaner. Waste is sucked into a tank to keep it from floating away.

21

Astronauts have a lot of
work to do in space. Many
astronauts study science.

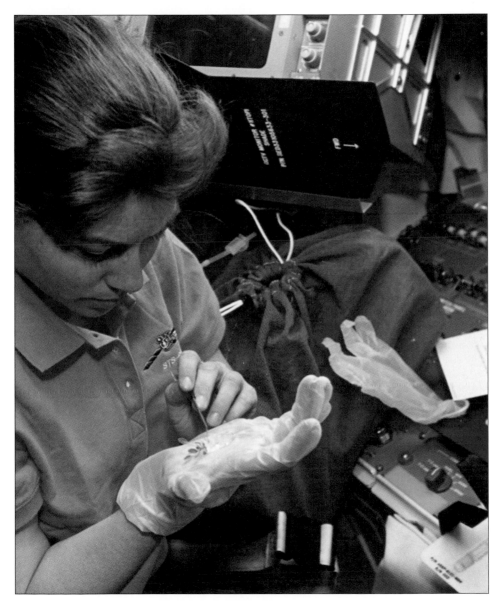

23

Astronauts like to have fun, too. Some astronauts have fun doing back flips.

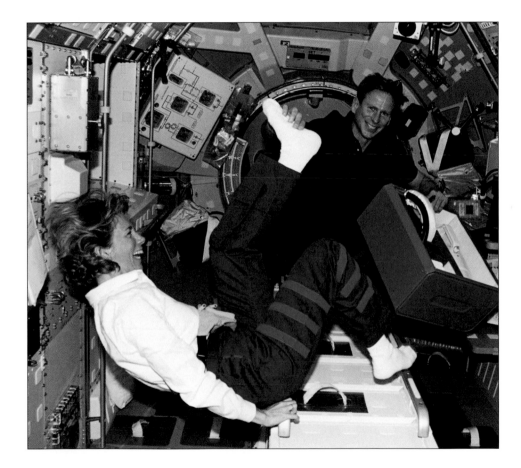

The crew enjoys looking at Earth. Our planet is beautiful from space.

Soon it is time to go to bed. Tired astronauts crawl into their sleeping bags.

Goodnight!

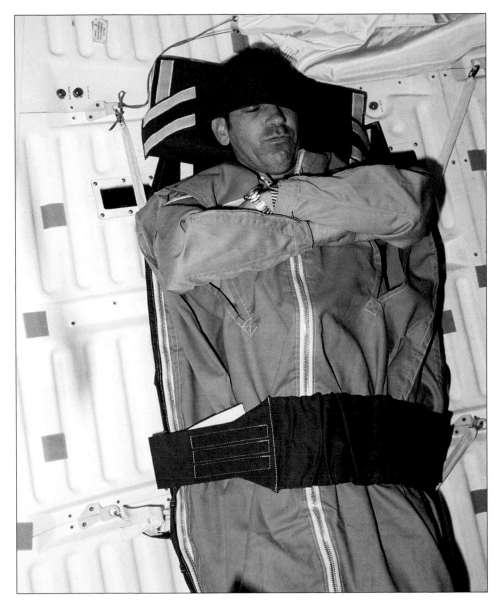

Words You Know

astronaut

floating

pouch

space shuttle

treadmill

31

Index

About the Author

Carmen Bredeson has written dozens of nonfiction books for children. She lives in Texas and enjoys traveling and doing research for her books.

Photo Credits